Save the Animals

Written by DEBORAH CHANCELLOR
Illustrated by DIANE EWEN

CRABTREE
PUBLISHING COMPANY
WWW.CRABTREEBOOKS.COM

Before, During, and After Reading Prompts

Activate Prior Knowledge and Make Predictions

Read the title of the book to the children and look at the illustrations. Ask children what they think the book may be about. Ask them questions related to the title, such as:

- What kinds of animals live in your community?
- What is an animal habitat? Can you think of some reasons an animal habitat might be destroyed?

During Reading

Stop at various points during reading and ask children questions related to the story:

- What happened to the woods in Leo's community? *(see pages 4–6)*
- What must animals do when they lose their habitat? What happens to animals that cannot adapt to new habitats? *(see pages 9–11)*
- What do Leo and his friends do to help save animals? *(see pages 18–20)*
- What happens at the Wildlife Action Day?

How will the school spend the money that was raised? *(see pages 22–24)*

After Reading

Look at the information panels, then talk together about endangered animals and their habitats. Ask children the following prompting questions:

- Can you name some animal habitats? *(see page 11)*
- Can you name some endangered animals? *(see pages 13, 21)*
- Why are forests cut down? *(see pages 5, 13)*
- What is happening to the ice at the North and South Poles? *(see pages 14–15)*
- How does saving energy and recycling help animal habitats? *(see page 17)*
- How do charities help animals? *(see page 25)*

Do the Quiz together *(see pages 28–29)*. Refer back to the information panels to find answers.

Crabtree Publishing Company

www.crabtreebooks.com   1-800-387-7650

Published in Canada
Crabtree Publishing
616 Welland Ave.
St. Catharines, Ontario
L2M 5V6

Published in the United States
Crabtree Publishing
PMB 59051
350 Fifth Avenue, 59th Floor
New York, New York 10118

PUBLISHED IN 2020 BY CRABTREE PUBLISHING COMPANY

First published in 2019 by Wayland (an imprint of Hachette Children's Group, part of Hodder and Stoughton)
Copyright © Hodder and Stoughton, 2019

Author: Deborah Chancellor
Illustrator: Diane Ewen
Editorial Director: Kathy Middleton
Editors: Sarah Peutrill, Ellen Rodger
Designer: Cathryn Gilbert
Print and production coordinator: Katherine Berti

Printed in the U.S.A./122019/CG20191101

Library and Archives Canada Cataloguing in Publication

Title: Save the animals / written by Deborah Chancellor ; illustrated by Diane Ewen.
Names: Chancellor, Deborah, author. | Ewen, Diane (Illustrator), illustrator.
Description: Series statement: Good to be green |
    Previously published: London: Wayland, 2019. | Includes index. |
    "A story about why it's important to help endangered animals".
Identifiers: Canadiana (print) 20190194340 |
    Canadiana (ebook) 20190194359 |
    ISBN 9780778772859 (hardcover) |
    ISBN 9780778772927 (softcover) |
    ISBN 9781427124722 (HTML)
Subjects: LCSH: Habitat conservation—Juvenile literature. |
    LCSH: Wildlife conservation—Juvenile literature. | LCSH: Sustainable living—Juvenile literature. | LCSH: Environmentalism—Juvenile literature.
Classification: LCC QH75 .C53 2020 | DDC j333.95/416—dc23

Library of Congress Cataloging-in-Publication Data

Names: Chancellor, Deborah, author. | Ewen, Diane (Illustrator), illustrator.
Title: Save the animals / written by Deborah Chancellor ;
    illustrated by Diane Ewen.
Description: New York : Crabtree Publishing Company, 2020. |
    Series: Good to be green |
    First published in Great Britain in 2019 by Wayland.
Identifiers: LCCN 2019043854 (print) | LCCN 2019043855 (ebook) |
    ISBN 9780778772859 (hardcover) |
    ISBN 9780778772927 (paperback) |
    ISBN 9781427124722 (ebook)
Subjects: LCSH: Wildlife conservation--Juvenile literature.
Classification: LCC QL83 .C46 2020 (print) | LCC QL83 (ebook) |
    DDC 333.95/4--dc23
LC record available at https://lccn.loc.gov/2019043854
LC ebook record available at https://lccn.loc.gov/2019043855

Save the Animals

A story about why it's important to help endangered animals.

Leo loved to play in the woods. But one day when he went there with Mom, all the trees had disappeared! Leo was very sad.

"But it was my favorite place to play!" cried Leo. "I made a fort there."

He thought about the wildlife in the woods. "Where are all the animals going to live?" he asked.

Mom sighed. She gave Leo a hug. "It's hard for animals when they lose their **habitat**," she said.

"Some animals will **adapt** and find somewhere else to live. Other animals can't do this so easily."

Leo thought for a moment.
"What happens to those
animals?" he asked.
"That's a big problem,"
said Mom. "In some
places, they die out
and are never seen again."

Different animals live in different habitats.
Examples of habitats include mountains, deserts,
rain forests, **coral reefs**, and the icy **poles**.
Human activities are harming many habitats,
putting the animals that live in them at risk.

Mountain

Snow leopard

Desert

Dama gazelle

Rain forest

Blue morpho butterfly

Coral reef

Spiny seahorse

Leo sighed. "That's terrible!" he said.
Mom nodded. "And small woods like this are
not the only habitats disappearing," she said.

"People cut down big
rain forests to get wood
or use the land for
mining or farming."

About one-fifth of the Amazon rain forest has been cut down in the last 50 years. The land is used mainly for cattle and soybean farms.

One out of ten of the world's animal **species** live in the Amazon. Some are **endangered**, like the poison dart frog.

Mom looked up at the sky.
"It's not just rain forests that are
disappearing," said Mom.
"So is the ice at the North
and South Poles."

"The **climate** around
the world is changing.
It is making the ice
at the poles melt."

Air pollution and **greenhouse gases** trap the Sun's rays near Earth. This heating up of the planet is called **global warming**. Temperatures near the North Pole are rising twice as fast as anywhere else on Earth, melting the ice that **Arctic** animals depend on.

"What can we do to stop this from happening?" Leo asked on the way home. "We can start by trying to cut air pollution," said Mom. "One way to do this is to save energy. That means burning less fuel, such as gas, and **recycling** more things."

When we recycle old things, we don't have to use energy to make new things. Cutting back on the amount of energy we use reduces air pollution. This slows down global warming and helps protect animal habitats.

Paper, cardboard, cans, and glass can be recycled.

Walking and cycling instead of driving a car saves energy.

The next day at school, Leo talked to his teacher, Mr. Green. "What can we do to take care of our planet and help save the animals?" Leo asked.

"You could put recycling boxes in all the classrooms," said Mr. Green.

"And turn off the lights when people leave them on."

"We should find out more about endangered animals and their habitats," said Mr. Green. The class painted pictures of animals at risk. Leo painted a tiger in a rain forest.

"Let's have a Wildlife Action Day," suggested Leo. "We could raise money to help animals in danger." Mr. Green thought this was a great idea.

All these animals and their habitats
are endangered.

The walrus hunts in the icy Arctic.

The hawksbill turtle
swims around colorful
coral reefs.

The orangutan
swings through
the rain forest.

The Wildlife Action Day was a big success. There was animal face painting and a game to guess the name of the gorilla.

Guess My Name!

Best of all was the pet competition.
The winner was a cat called Ziggy.
Ziggy was fierce and looked just
like a tiger.

At the end of the day, Leo helped Mr. Green count the money. Leo smiled. "We've got enough to adopt a tiger!" he said.

Wildlife charities work hard to protect animals and habitats. You can give them money to "adopt" an animal that is in danger of becoming **extinct**. You don't actually get to keep the animal! Your money helps the charity provide a safe **conservation** area, where the animal can live and have babies.

Leo couldn't wait to tell Mom about Ziggy the Tiger. Mom smiled. "I'm so proud of you!" she said.

Mom and Leo made a new fort in their
yard to celebrate. Leo knew they would
protect their own backyard habitat.

Quiz time

Which of these things are true? Read the book again to find out!

(Cover up the answers on page 29.)

1. All animals adapt easily to new habitats.

2. People are harming animal habitats.

3. One in 50 animal species lives in the Amazon rain forest.

4. Ice never melts near the North Pole.

5. Recycling and saving energy help to save animal habitats.

Answers

1. **False**  Some animal species are dying out because their habitats are disappearing, and they can't adapt to survive. *(See pages 8–9, 10–11)*

2. **True**  People are cutting down rain forests, and pollution is damaging many animal habitats, such as the Arctic. *(See pages 10–11, 12–13, 14–15)*

3. **False** Amazingly, one in ten of all the world's animal species lives in the Amazon rain forest. *(See pages 12–13)*

4. **False**  Temperatures are rising faster near the North Pole than anywhere else on Earth. This is melting the ice. *(See pages 14–15)*

5. **True**  When we save energy and recycle, we reduce pollution and conserve natural resources, which helps protect animal habitats. *(See pages 16–17)*

Get active

In the story, Leo and his friends put on a Wildlife Action Day at school to raise money for a wildlife charity. Ask your teacher if you can do something similar at your school. Ask your family and friends to help.

Find some pictures of endangered animals, if possible in their natural habitats. Make a poster to tell people about animals in danger.

Air pollution adds to global warming and climate change. Find out which animals are in danger because of melting ice. Write a poem about an endangered polar animal.

It's good to recycle paper and cardboard. It saves the energy and wood that are needed to produce new paper products. Ask at home or school for help to increase the amount of paper and cardboard you recycle or use again.

A note about sharing this book

The *Good to Be Green* series provides a starting point for further discussion on important environmental issues, such as pollution, climate change, and endangered wildlife. Each topic is relevant to both children and adults.

Save the Animals!

This story explores some issues surrounding the problem of habitat loss and endangered animals. *Save the Animals!* contains practical suggestions for how to protect animal species and the places where they live. For example, children can help raise money to support the work of wildlife and environment charities. The information panels in the book introduce the important issues of global warming and climate change, explaining their causes and how they affect animal habitats. The story and nonfiction elements in *Save the Animals!* encourage the reader to conclude that we should all be aware of how humans impact animal habitats, and learn about ways we can take action to help minimize this impact.

How to use the book

Adults can share this story with individuals or a group of children, and use it as a starting point for discussion. Illustrations support text to help raise confidence in new readers. Repetition is used to reinforce understanding. For example, the phrases "Mom sighed" and "Leo sighed" are found at points throughout the book. Later, the positive outcome of the Wildlife Action Day transforms this negative phrase into "Mom smiled" and "Leo smiled."

The story introduces vocabulary relevant to endangered animals and habitats, such as: *climate, conservation, coral reef, endangered, extinct, global warming, greenhouse gases, habitat, pollution, rain forest, recycle*, and *species*. Some of the vocabulary in the story and information panels will be unfamiliar to the reader. These words are in bold text, and they are defined in the glossary on page 32. When reading the story for the first time, refer to the glossary with the children.

There is also an index on page 32. Encourage children to use the index when you are talking about the book. For example, ask them to use the index to find the pages where rain forests are mentioned (pages 11, 12, 13, 14, 20, 21). This useful research skill can teach children that information can be found in books as well as searched for on the Internet, with a responsible adult.

Glossary

adapt To get used to living in a new situation or place

air pollution Harmful chemicals that make the air dirty

Arctic The area around the North Pole

climate The pattern of weather over a period of time

conservation Work done to protect a habitat, living thing, or a historic or artistic object or building

coral reef A structure in warm, shallow seas, made of tiny animals

endangered Rare and in danger of dying out

extinct A species that is dead and gone forever

global warming The rise in Earth's temperature, caused by air pollution, or gases trapped in Earth's atmosphere

greenhouse gases Gases such as carbon dioxide and methane that trap the Sun's heat near Earth

habitat The place where a living thing is usually found and prefers to live

mining Digging natural material, such as coal, out of the ground

Poles The North Pole and the South Pole are the places on the surface of Earth that are the farthest points north and south

rain forest A thick, tropical woodland where it rains a lot

recycling Making something used into something useful again

species A group of living things that are alike in many ways and can have babies

Index